GETTYSBURG
The Delaplaine
2021
Long Weekend Guide

NO BUSINESS HAS PAID A SINGLE PENNY OR GIVEN *ANYTHING* TO BE INCLUDED IN THIS BOOK.

Andrew Delaplaine

Senior Writer – James Cubby

Gramercy Park Press
New York London Paris

Please submit corrections, additions or comments
to andrewdelaplaine@mac.com

GETTYSBURG
The Delaplaine
Long Weekend Guide

TABLE OF CONTENTS

Chapter 1
WHY GETTYSBURG?

I've always thought it ironic that the famous battle fought here in 1863 that determined the fate of the Civil War was waged over the three days of July 1-3, ending just before our Independence Day.

So close did the Confederates come to winning when Pickett's Charge breached the

Union line on Cemetery Ridge that if they had not been repulsed, the Confederates could easily have called the following day, July 4, their own Independence Day. It's not for nothing that this point in the battle is called the "high-water mark of the Confederacy."

General Lee's army retreated the following day back into Virginia. Though the awful war would go on for two more years and see countless more dead, this was the turning point.

A few months after the battle, a military cemetery was dedicated here. A famous speaker, Edward Everett, delivered a long-winded two-hour oration before President Lincoln delivered his slightly more famous address. In fact, Everett is only known now because his (forgotten) speech preceded Lincoln's, which went into the history books as one of the most eloquent speeches ever made.

Everett's oration (that ran to 13,607 words) started with this:

"Standing beneath this serene sky, overlooking these broad fields now reposing from the labors of the waning year, the mighty Alleghenies dimly towering before us, the graves of our brethren beneath our feet, it is with hesitation that I raise my poor voice to break the eloquent silence of God and Nature…"

Two hours later, it ended with:

"But they, I am sure, will join us in saying, as we bid farewell to the dust of these martyr-heroes, that wheresoever throughout the civilized world the accounts of this great warfare are read, and down to the latest period of recorded time, in the glorious annals of our common country, there will be no brighter page than that which relates the Battles of Gettysburg."

Those present must have been thankful it was November. Imagine having to stand out in the open field in summer and listen to this guy.

Lincoln's address—only three paragraphs, ran like this:

"Four score and seven years ago our fathers brought forth on this continent a new nation, conceived in liberty, and dedicated to the proposition that all men are created equal.

"Now we are engaged in a great civil war, testing whether that nation, or any nation so conceived and so dedicated, can long endure. We are met on a great battlefield of that war. We have come to dedicate a portion of that field, as a final resting place for those who here gave their lives that that nation might live. It is altogether fitting and proper that we should do this.

"But, in a larger sense, we can not dedicate, we can not consecrate, we can not hallow this ground. The brave men, living and dead, who struggled here, have consecrated it, far above our poor power to add or detract. The world will little note, nor long remember what we say here, but it can never forget what they did here. It is for us the living, rather, to be dedicated here to the unfinished work which they who fought here have thus far so nobly advanced. It is rather for us to be here dedicated to the great task remaining before us—that from these honored dead we take increased devotion to that cause for which they gave the last full measure of devotion—that we here highly resolve that these dead shall not have died in vain—that this nation, under God, shall have a new birth of freedom—and that government of the people, by the people, for the people, shall not perish from the earth."

I have visited several Civil War battlefields in my life. This is the one that haunts me still, maybe because it was so important. It's to this day the biggest battle fought on land on this Continent.

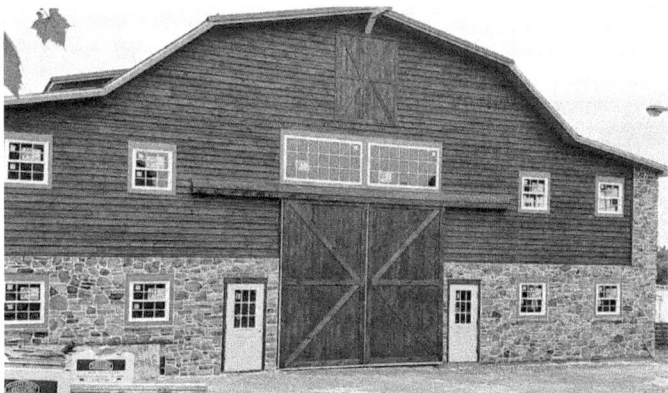

Chapter 2
GETTING ABOUT

You will need a car unless you want to take a guided tour or see the battlefield by bike or Segway.

CAR: There are numerous places where you can pull off the road and get out to walk onto the battlefield. You can gets maps (or even a helpful CD) that will assist as you figure out what's where. I might also suggest studying the battle a little before you get here. It makes a substantial difference.

BIKE: Rent a bike and get a little closer to the action. Rentals available in Gettysburg.

SEGWAY: Segway rentals are also available at:
SegTours
22 Springs Ave., Gettysburg: 717-253-7987
www.segtours.com
They offer tours that might be of interest to you, especially if you get one of their tour guides.

TOUR BUS
GETTYSBURG TOUR CENTER
778 Baltimore St., Gettysburg, 877-680-8687
www.gettysburgbattlefieldtours.com
Although this method sticks you inside an air-conditioned bus and removes you from the battlefield, it's a quick way to get through the whole affair. The guides narrating the tour are all licensed. In good weather, they have open-air double-deckers, so try to get on the top level if you can.

Chapter 3
WHERE TO STAY

1863 INN OF GETTYSBURG
516 Baltimore St, Gettysburg, 717-334-6211
www.1863innofgettysburg.com
Located in the historic district, this five-story Inn offers 110 spacious guestrooms and suites. Amenities include: Flat screen TVs, complimentary parking, complimentary breakfast and Wi-Fi access, outdoor pool and fitness center. Pet friendly rooms are available. Near local attractions.

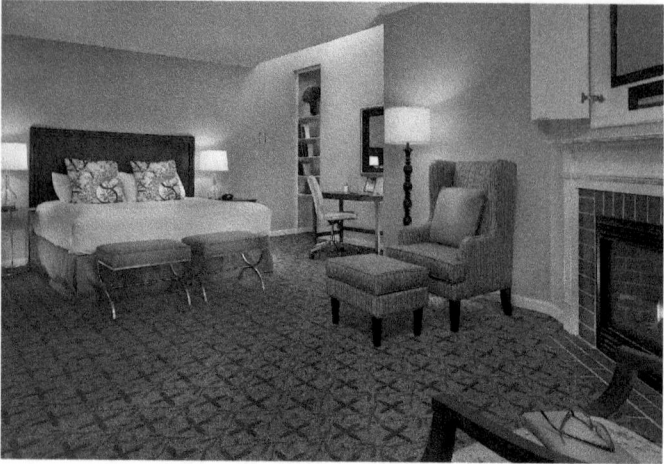

THE GETTYSBURG HOTEL
1 Lincoln Square, Gettysburg, 717 337-2000
www.hotelgettysburg.com
Located in the heart of historic downtown
Gettysburg, this renovated 1797 hotel features
119 guestrooms and suites. Amenities include:
complimentary high speed wireless Internet,
fitness center access, rooftop swimming pool, flat
screen TVs, and onsite dining. Conveniently
located to Gettysburg National Parks and local
attractions.

HILTON GARDEN INN GETTYSBURG
1061 York Rd, Gettysburg, 717-334-2040
http://hiltongardeninn3.hilton.com/en/hotels/penn
sylvania/hilton-garden-inn-gettysburg-
MDTGHGI/index.html

This Inn offers a variety of spacious guestrooms and suites with elegant furnishings and modern conveniences. Amenities include: LCD TV, Fitness Center, indoor pool and whirlpool, and complimentary high-speed Internet access. On-site restaurant.

INN AT HERR RIDGE
900 Chambersburg Rd., 800-362-9849
https://www.innatherrridge.com/
Built in 1815, this former Civil War hospital has been transformed into an enchanting inn with 17 distinctive guest rooms and suites (all with individual décor). As old as the place might be, it's got all the modern amenities: Complimentary Wi-Fi, flat-screen TVs, Keurig coffeemakers and fireplaces. Many have whirlpool tubs, and some

have balconies. On-site French-American restaurant, an informal grill eatery (see separate listings), a wine cellar (boasting some 6,000 bottles), a spa, and a Rooftop Terrace with views of the battlefields. Complimentary parking. Kids 12 and over are welcome. Minutes from downtown Gettysburg and 3 miles from the Gettysburg National Cemetery and the battlefields in Gettysburg National Military Park.

INN AT LINCOLN SQUARE
12 Lincoln Square, Gettysburg, 717-353-2471
www.innatlincolnsquare.com
Located in the heart of Gettysburg, this inn features a beautifully decorated interior. The Inn offers five luxurious living quarters: three suites

and two town houses. Conveniently located near attractions like the historic David Wills House, shopping and restaurants.

THE JAMES GETTYS HOTEL
27 Chambersburg St, Gettysburg, 717-337-1334
www.jamesgettyshotel.com
Located in historic downtown Gettysburg, this hotel was built in 1804 and retains its classic charm. The hotel features 12 tastefully appointed suites. Amenities include: Complimentary Wi-Fi, cable TV, complimentary continental breakfast, and free parking.

THE LODGES AT GETTYSBURG

685 Camp Gettysburg Rd, Gettysburg, 717-642-2500

www.gettysburgaccommodations.com

This elegant 63-acre private retreat is set on one of the most beautiful ridge lines in Gettysburg. The spacious private accommodations feature full kitchenettes, private bathrooms, private porches, flat screen TVs, and high speed internet access. The Lodges overlook the historic Gettysburg battlefields and Hunter Lake, which is stocked with bass and other game fish.

WYNDHAM GETTYSBURG
95 Presidential Cir, Gettysburg, 717-339-0020
www.gatewaygettysburg.com
This Wyndham hotel offers old-world charm with modern conveniences. The Wyndham features beautifully appointed guestrooms and suites. Amenities include: Indoor swimming pool, spa whirlpools, fitness center, complimentary Wi-Fi, daily newspaper, and complimentary bottled water. On-site movie theater. Smoke-free environment.

Chapter 4
WHERE TO EAT

1863 RESTAURANT
WYNDHAM HOTEL
95 Presidential Cir, Gettysburg, 717-339-0020
www.1863restaurantandlounge.com/
CUISINE: American (New)
DRINKS: Full Bar
SERVING: Breakfast, Lunch & Dinner
PRICE RANGE: $$
NEIGHBORHOOD: Near Downtown
Located in the modern Wyndham Hotel, the
formal dining room here is very lovely with its
light pastel walls and elegant white tablecloth
service you won't find in the numerous ultra-
simple eateries that mostly populate the town.
But I prefer the more casual bar area, whether
you sit at the bar itself or over against the wall at
a table. It's just as charming. The "bistro-ish"
menu does go a little beyond the usual American
classics, including all-day-breakfast, build-your-

own-Angus-hamburgers, several steak cuts and a good French dip, but with a Poppyseed roll, as well as King and Queen Cut Prime Rib. Daily lunch specials are definitely worth a look.

DOBBIN HOUSE TAVERN
89 Steinwehr Ave, Gettysburg, 717-334-2100
www.dobbinhouse.com
CUISINE: Colonial, Continental
DRINKS: Full Bar
SERVING: Breakfast, Lunch, Dinner
PRICE RANGE: $$
Listed on the National Register of Historic Places, this colonial restaurant offers candlelit elegance. The food is superior and the service excellent. Six historic rooms are available for

your dining pleasure. Homemade breads.
Reservations advised.

ERNIE'S TEXAS LUNCH
58 Chambersburg St, Gettysburg, 717-334-1970
www.ernies-texas-lunch.com
CUISINE: American, Diner
DRINKS: Beer & Wine Only
SERVING: Breakfast, Lunch, Dinner; Closed
Sun
PRICE RANGE: $
This is an old-time lunch counter equipped with
booths. Menu staples are hot dogs and fries.

**FARNSWORTH HOUSE INN &
RESTAURANT**
401 Baltimore St, Gettysburg, 717-334-8838
www.farnsworthhouseinn.com
CUISINE: American

DRINKS: Beer & Wine Only
SERVING: Dinner
PRICE RANGE: $$
Great period dining rooms and good food. Menu favorites include: BBQ Sandwich and Crab stuffed flounder. Historic feeling, memorabilia displayed from movie *Gettysburg*, and servers are dressed in period costume.

FOOD 101
101 Chambersburg St, Gettysburg, 717-334-6080
www.food101gettysburg.com
CUISINE: American (New)/Pizza
DRINKS: No Booze, but you can BYOB from across the street where there's a store.
SERVING: Lunch & Dinner (till 8, or 9 on weekends)
PRICE RANGE: $$
NEIGHBORHOOD: Downtown
Cute little café in an old red brick building downtown that looks like it dates back to the Civil War, but I don't think it actually does. Inside, it's quite modern, with black-and-white checkered tile floor, stainless-edged diner style tables, bright cheerful art adorning the walls. Menu is strictly all-American fare, with salads, sandwiches, burgers, pizza and a few heavier entrée items like rack of lamb or "bistro steak." Stick with the lighter items, although I have to admit the pan-roasted chicken was very tasty,

with apples and Yukon potatoes, onions. Gluten-free options.

GARRYOWEN IRISH PUB
126 Chambersburg St, Gettysburg. 717-337-2719
www.garryowenirishpub.net
CUISINE: Irish
DRINKS: Full Bar
SERVING: Lunch & Dinner
PRICE RANGE: $$
Typical Irish fare with Guinness on draft. Menu favorites include: Shepherd's Pie and Irish onion soup. Live music. Specialty nights.

GETTYSBURG EDDIE'S
217 Steinwehr Ave, Gettysburg, 717-334-1100

www.gettysburgeddies.com
CUISINE: American (New)
DRINKS: Full Bar
SERVING: Lunch & Dinner
PRICE RANGE: $$
NEIGHBORHOOD: Gettysburg
Casual tavern and sports bar dedicated to local baseball Hall of Famer Edward Plank. Red-brick walls are covered with old period baseball pictures and other sports memorabilia. A fried-food junkie's dream menu. Menu favorites: Santa Fe Strip Steak and Portobello Crab Melt, but they have one of those menus that go on and on (and even further on), with pizzas, cheesesteaks; 4 different soups; Nachos (of course); a half dozen salads; fried baskets (chicken tenders, fried shrimp); burgers and a dozen other sandwiches; some seafood selections, even pasta. *Whew!* They boast a half-dozen large screen LCD TVs to watch the games.

GETTYSBURG FAMILY RESTAURANT
1275 York Rd Ste 5, Gettysburg, 717-337-2700
https://www.facebook.com/pages/category/Diner/
Gettysburg-Family-Restaurant-
117493138270095/
CUISINE: American (Traditional)
DRINKS: No Booze
SERVING: Breakfast, Lunch & Dinner, Brunch
PRICE RANGE: $
NEIGHBORHOOD: York Road

Located in a boring strip mall is this uninspiring old-fashioned eatery that offers down-home old-fashioned meals. Nothing fancy, just basic good food. And cheap. Breakfast is their specialty, but the fried chicken is hard to beat as well. Great sandwiches. This is where you come when you're hung over or just don't want to deal with the real world for an hour or two.

HUNT'S CAFE
61 Steinwehr Ave, Gettysburg. 717-334-4787
https://www.facebook.com/pages/Hunts-Battlefield-Fries-and-Cafe/110327159002185
CUISINE: Cheesecake, Sandwiches
DRINKS: No Booze
SERVING: Lunch & Dinner
PRICE RANGE: $

Interesting décor but great food. Menu favorites include great burgers and real French fries. Good spot for breakfast. Try the Sugar and Cinnamon French toast. Walls are covered with memorabilia.

INN AT HERR RIDGE
900 Chambersburg Rd., 800-362-9849
https://www.innatherrridge.com/
CUISINE: American
DRINKS: Full Bar
SERVING: Lunch, Dinner
PRICE RANGE: $$
This old inn and tavern dating back to 1815 (but thoroughly modernized) has a fine dining restaurant in it (with over 6,000 bottles in its cellar that was good enough to get a nod from the 'Wine Spectator') that's well worth a visit, especially if you're sick and tired of all the fried

junk food to be found in so many of the local eateries and want something a little more special. (OK, a *lot* more special.) In good weather, try to get an outdoor table. Nothing terribly clever or original about the American menu, but what's here is of a high quality. Blue Crab & Corn Chowder; Lamb Shank (braised 9 hours with veggies in a rich savory Malbec); Pan-seared Scallops. There's a prix-fixe menu that I would recommend, especially if you're getting a nice bottle of wine.

LA BELLA ITALIA
402 York St, Gettysburg, 717-334-1978
www.labellaitaliagettysburg.com
Here you'll find great Italian food and delicious pizza. Menu favorites include: Baked Stuffed Shells and Spaghetti w/Meat Sauce.
CUISINE: Pizza, Italian
DRINKS: Beer & Wine
SERVING: Lunch, Dinner
PRICE RANGE: $$

LINCOLN DINER
32 Carlisle St, Gettysburg, 717-334-3900
www.thelincolndiner.com
CUISINE: American, Diner
DRINKS: No Booze
SERVING: Breakfast, Lunch, Dinner
PRICE RANGE: $
Typical diner fare available 24 hours a day. Great spot for breakfast (served all day).
Friendly service.

THE LIVERY
INN AT HERR RIDGE

900 Chambersburg Rd, Gettysburg, 717-334-4598
https://www.innatherrridge.com/
www.liverybarandgrille.com
CUISINE: American
DRINKS: Full Bar
SERVING: Breakfast, Lunch, Dinner
PRICE RANGE: $$

This is the "casual" dining option at this historic inn & B&B which is right across the road from the battlefield where the First Day was fought in the great Civil War battle that put this sleepy little hamlet on the map, and likely the reason you're here at all. Nice menu featuring everything from Alaskan snow crab legs to their famous Dry Rubbed Jumbo Chicken Wings; Maryland Crab Soup; Chesapeake Crab Dip in a sourdough bread bowl; lots of sandwiches, salads, a big selection of burgers. A big choice of over 90 craft and micro brews. Breakfast served all day. Live entertainment on weekends. Video games and pool table.

MASON DIXON DISTILLERY & RESTAURANT
331 E Water St, Gettysburg, 717-398-3385
www.masondixondistillery.com/
CUISINE: American (New)
DRINKS: Full Bar
SERVING: Lunch & Dinner; Closed Mon & Tues.

PRICE RANGE: $$
NEIGHBORHOOD: Gettysburg
Casual eatery and distillery located in a 100-year-old former furniture factory with a bare bones interior of old red brick walls, rough-hewn wooden pillars holding up the roof, basic backless bar stools. The level of the food quality is surprisingly more elevated than the rustic surroundings. (Well, I was surprised at any rate!) Short Ribs Eggs Benedict; Pastrami Hash (excellent, by the way); Raisin Pecan French Toast; Steak Tip Sandwich; Monte Christo; great gooey Grilled Cheese. All their liquor is made from scratch onsite. Crafted cocktails, of course.

MONTEZUMA
225 Buford Ave, Gettysburg, 717-334-7750
www.montezumamex.com
CUISINE: Mexican
DRINKS: No Booze
SERVING: Lunch, Dinner
PRICE RANGE: $
Mexican eatery offering typical fare. Menu favorites include: enchiladas supremas and pollo asado (chicken cutlet). No booze so it's BYOB.

ROOFTOP TERRACE
INN AT HERR RIDGE
900 Chambersburg Rd., 800-362-9849
https://www.innatherrridge.com/
CUISINE: American

DRINKS: Full Bar
SERVING: Lunch, Dinner
PRICE RANGE: $$
I've mentioned the Inn at Herr Ridge elsewhere, but want you to be sure not to overlook their rooftop terrace. They have a complete menu up here atop the historic inn and tavern. Well worth checking out. Great view of the battlefield.

SIDNEY WILLOUGHBY RUN
730 Chambersburg Rd., Gettysburg. 717-334-3774
www.restaurantsidney.com
CUISINE: American
DRINKS: Full Bar
SERVING: Lunch & Dinner
PRICE RANGE: $$$
This is renowned chef Neil Annis' second restaurant. His menu features small, elegant bites

made with fresh, local ingredients. Menu favorites include: Cheddar and goat cheese macaroni with chunks of Maryland blue crab. Impressive wine list. Great service.

WEST SIDE DINER
51 West St, Gettysburg, 717-334-0172
No Website
CUISINE: Diner
DRINKS: No Booze
SERVING: Breakfast, Lunch & Dinner (7 am to 8 pm)
PRICE RANGE: $
NEIGHBORHOOD: Lakeview
Completely unassuming classic diner offers typical American fare and comfort food. A humble outpost for classic breakfast dishes, sandwiches & comfort-food entrees. Breakfast served all day (which is the best thing about it).

Chapter 5
NIGHTLIFE

THE APPALACHIAN BREWING COMPANY

70 Presidential Circle, Gettysburg, 717-398-2419
259 Steinwehr Avenue, Gettysburg, 717-334-2200

www.abcbrew.com

The brewing system's copper tanks below the cozy wooden bar can be toured by appointment during the day. At night, try one of its 16 draft beers on tap, including a seasonal craft ale like Hinterland Hefe Weizen. Has a good brewpub menu as well.

RELIANCE MINE SALOON
380 Steinwehr Ave, Gettysburg, 717 334-1103

http://reliancemine.com/
This unique saloon features a dark mine décor that's a popular hangout of Gettysburg tour guides. Nothing fancy here. Closed Sundays.

Chapter 6
WHAT TO SEE & DO

ADAMS COUNTY WINERY
251 Peach Tree Rd, Orrtanna. 717-334-4631
www.adamscountywinery.com
A 1860s red barn in where you can taste up to
six wines, including a sweet Niagara, for free.

THE DAVID WILLS HOUSE
8 Lincoln Square, Gettysburg. 717-334-2499
www.nps.gov/gett/planyourvisit/david-wills-house.htm
This historic house features five museum galleries and two recreated rooms. This is the house where Abraham Lincoln and 37 other dignitaries visited the evening before the Soldier's National Cemetery Dedication ceremony in 1863. You can also view the room where Lincoln finished his immortal Gettysburg Address. Free Admission.

EISENHOWER NATIONAL HISTORIC SITE

1195 Baltimore Pike, Gettysburg, 717-338-9114
www.nps.gov/eise
Located adjacent to the Gettysburg Battlefield,
Eisenhower National Historic Site was the home
and farm of General and President Dwight D.
Eisenhower which served as a weekend retreat
and meeting place for world leaders. Located
adjacent to the Gettysburg Battlefield, the farm
served the President as a weekend retreat and a
meeting place for world leaders. Visit via shuttle
buses from the Gettysburg National Military Park
Museum and Visitor Center. Admission fee.

GETTYSBURG COLLEGE

300 N Washington St, Gettysburg. 717-337-6300

www.gettysburg.edu
Founded in 1832, Gettysburg College sits on 200 bucolic acres north of the town's center. Walk among the mostly brick Georgian and Victorian buildings and stop at the stately, white Pennsylvania Hall, an administrative building that was a signal corps station and field hospital for Union and Confederate troops during the battle. Sit in the Adirondack chairs on its expansive lawn.

GETTYSBURG DIORAMA
241 Steinwehr Ave, Gettysburg, 717-334-6408
www.gettysburgdiorama.com
The Battle of Gettysburg is presented with narration across a three-dimensional landscape. This is the largest military diorama in the U.S.

The diorama features over 20,000 hand painted soldiers, horses, cannons, and buildings. The museum also has a large display of historical items and an impressive display of Civil War paintings.
Open daily. Admission fee.

GETTYSBURG HERITAGE CENTER
297 Steinwehr Ave, Gettysburg, 717-334-6245
www.gettysburgmuseum.com
Popular with Civil War aficionados. This museum offers the story of the Civil War era with life-size dioramas. Highlights include: Abraham Lincoln's Gettysburg Address. Self-guide tour tells the history of the Civil War including the Battle of Gettysburg. Admission fee.

GETTYSBURG MAJESTIC THEATER

25 Carlisle St, Gettysburg, 717-337-8200
www.gettysburgmajestic.org
Opened in Gettysburg in 1925 as the largest
vaudeville and silent movie theater in south-
central Pennsylvania, the theater has recently
undergone a $20 million restoration. Open to the
public with entertainment schedule that includes
award-winning comics, Broadway, dance, and
films.

GETTYSBURG NATIONAL MILITARY PARK

1195 Baltimore Pike (Route 97), 717-334-1124
www.nps.gov/gett/
Gettysburg National Military Park spans 5,989
acres of woodlands, farmlands, craggy ridges and
sloping valleys, with more than 1,300 monuments
erected by the battle's veterans and state
governments. Start at McPherson Ridge, where,

early in the morning of July 1, 1863, fighting broke out between Union cavalry and Confederate infantry. Then drive south to Little Round Top, the craggy hill that Union soldiers, in a downhill bayonet charge, defended against Confederate troops. At the High Water Mark, look out on the open field where nearly 12,000 Confederate infantrymen crossed in a mile-long front known as Pickett's Charge. Cross the road to Soldiers' National Cemetery, where about 3,500 Union soldiers lay buried, 1,632 in unmarked graves.

THE GETTYSBURG NATIONAL PARK SERVICE MUSEUM AND VISITOR CENTER
1195 Baltimore Pike, Gettysburg, 717-334-1124
www.nps.gov/gett/
The museum offers a variety of information on the Civil War through short videos, photographs and artifacts. The park includes 26 miles of road

that visitors travel by car. CDs of self-guided tours are available. Two-hour bus tours are also available. Reservations are made online at tickets.gettsburgfoundation.org (at least 3 days in advance). Admission fee for museum.

GHOSTS OF GETTYSBURG
271 Baltimore St, Gettysburg, 717-337-0445
www.ghostsofgettysburg.com
Discover the ghosts of Gettysburg in a variety of guided tours: Baltimore Street Tour, Bus Tour-Steinwehr Avenue Tour, and Carlisle Street Tour. Since the Battle of Gettysburg there have been legions of sightings and stories.   The knowledgeable guides share some of the many stories during the tours. Fee.

HOLLABAUGH BROS. INC.
545 Carlisle Rd, Biglerville, 717-677-8412
www.hollabaughbros.com
Well-known family farm that retails fresh fruits,
vegetables, jarred and baked goods, and gift
baskets.

JENNIE WADE HOUSE
548 Baltimore St, Gettysburg, 717-334-4100
www.jennie-wade-house.com
The home of the only Gettysburg civilian killed
during the Battle of Gettysburg. Now a shrine to
the former occupant, the house remains like it
was 100 years ago with authentic furnishings.
Costumed

guides tell the history of the home. Gift shop features souvenirs and collectibles. Regularly scheduled tours. Admission fee.

LINCOLN'S LOST TREASURE
56 East Middle St, Gettysburg, 800-838-3006
www.lincolnslosttreasure.com
This is a LIVE 2 ½-hour adventure that takes you through the streets of historic Downtown Gettysburg. This is an interactive scavenger hunt to uncover a lost secret. Groups of 6-8 people actively participate in this adventure, decoding cryptic clues and dodging FBI agents, traveling through the streets of town, stopping at historical landmarks and finally discovering the final clue in Lincoln's Gettysburg Address. Admission fee.

THE MUSSELMAN LIBRARY
300 North Washington St, Gettysburg, 717-337-7024
http://www.gettysburg.edu/library
Musselman Library is the library of Gettysburg College, an educational and research library. Library often features student-curated exhibitions.

THE SHRIVER HOUSE MUSEUM
309 Baltimore St, Gettysburg. 717-337-2800
www.shriverhouse.org
This award-winning Civil War museum celebrates the civilian experience of the Battle of Gettysburg. This story of the Shriver family who settled in the area in the 1700s. Today the home of George and Hettie Shriver remains for the most part the same as it did in 1860. Guides in

period dress share the story of the Shriver's experience during the Battle of Gettysburg. Visitors are allowed to tour all four floors of the house including the attic. Nominal fee.

TOUR BUS
GETTYSBURG TOUR CENTER
GETTYSBURG BATTLEFIELD TOURS
778 Baltimore St., Gettysburg, 877-680-8687
www.gettysburgbattlefieldtours.com
Although this method sticks you inside an air-conditioned bus and removes you from the battlefield, it's a quick way to get through the whole affair. The guides narrating the tour are all licensed. In good weather, they have open-air double-deckers, so try to get on the top level if you can.

Chapter 7
SHOPPING & SERVICES

THE GETTYSBURG FARMER'S MARKET
Lincoln Square, Gettysburg. No Phone
www.gettysburgfarmmarket.com
Located in the center of Gettysburg on the historic Lincoln Square. The merchants offer a variety of locally grown produce, products and services including: herbs, breads, plants, flowers, soaps, art, jams & jellies, crafts, fruits & vegetables. Saturdays from 7 a.m. to noon.

GETTYSBURG GIFT CENTER
297 Steinwehr Avenue, Gettysburg, 717-334-6245
www.GettysburgMuseum.com
Known as Gettysburg's largest and finest gift shop, this shop offers a wide variety of gifts, books, art, home décor, collectibles, souvenirs, apparel, games and toys. Has a big online store.

LORD NELSON'S GALLERY
27 Chambersburg St, Gettysburg, 800-664-9797
www.lordnelsons.com
Located a half a block from Lincoln Square, this
gallery features art, gifts, and accessories. Half of
the store is dedicated to Eastern Indian/Frontier
art of the French & Indian War period.

ROUND BARN FARM MARKET
298 Cashtown Rd, Biglerville. 717-334-1984
www.roundbarngettysburg.com
 Located in a 1914 white barn in Biglerville. The
family owned company sells fresh produce,

cheeses, snacks and its own pickled vegetables and jams.

SWEEET!
100 Baltimore St, Gettysburg, 717-339-0039
www.sweeetgettysburg.com
NEIGHBORHOOD: Lincoln Square
A must-see in Gettysburg, this unique candy store serves up sweet memories, vintage candy, and candy in almost any type of package you want.

INDEX

<u>NOTES</u>

NOTES

<u>NOTES</u>

NOTES

NOTES

NOTES

www.ingramcontent.com/pod-product-compliance
Lightning Source LLC
LaVergne TN
LVHW021622080426
835510LV00019B/2723